Change Management for the 21st Century

and Beyond

By

Iris Billy

© 2014

Dedication

Dedicated to the three top women in my life, my mother Mary Billy who was always my inspiration and without her love and dedication I would not be the woman I am today (RIP my angel). To my sister Suzette who has always encouraged me in my educational pursuits, and my sister in faith, Dr. Ruth Tappin, who continues to inspire, assist, and encourage me in all scholarly attempts.

About this Book

This book discusses the best practices for initiating organizational change and evaluates the likely influences of leader-follower relationships on the change management strategy. For this purpose, this book will provide a brief background about the concepts of organizational change management and theories that deals with leader-follower relationships, so as to develop the basis of arguments in this regard. The types of change that will be referred to in this book will relate to premeditated, far-reaching, radical, and long-term change; it will not address the day-to-day, incidental changes that occur in organizations. In sum this book will analyze organizational change, leader-follower relationships, and best practices for initiating change management strategies.

TABLE OF CONTENTS

CHAPTER 1: Introduction

Organizational Change

Organizations are changing on a constant basis due to globalization, changing customer needs, the introduction of new technology, restructuring, mergers or process improvements; therefore change is an unavoidable aspect of today's working environments (Davis & Marquis, 2005; Preget, 2013). According to Hayes (2010) and Raineri (2011) organizational change happens when transformations are required to align an organization with changing trends, and change management is the strategy to consistently manage changes that are introduced in an organization.

Different change models have been introduced in the literature but since organizational change is a piecemeal process, there has not been one coherent model for managing organizational change. According to Blake & Mosley (2011) and Giannantonio & Hurley-Hanson (2011), as far back as 1911 the literature has recommended scientific techniques for managing change. For example, Frederick Taylor (1856 – 1915) conceptualized the key concepts associated with the scientific management of organizational change in his book *Scientific Management* (circa 1911). Explaining Taylor's perspective of scientific change management, Nelson (1980) and Gumusluoglu and Ilsev (2009) opined that organizations pursuing an analytical and scientifically systematic approach to change management would provide the best opportunity for successful organizational change.

In this paradigm, for an organization to achieve the best results when orchestrating change management, there must be a systematic collection of data and the collected data must be meticulously analyzed, and applied rigorously, if not rigidly. In other words, effective change management mandated the scientific evaluation of the practicability of the change before introducing the change to subordinates (Nelson, 1980). Since the last century, programs that attempted to address organizational change more scientifically included Total Quality Management (TQM), Business Process Re-engineering (BPR) and the implementation of information and communication technologies (Harwood, 2012, p.748). However, the success rates of these programs have been extremely low and failure rates routinely exceeded 60% to 80%

(Harwood, 2012). This is because employees routinely resist change

(Davis & Marquis, 2005).

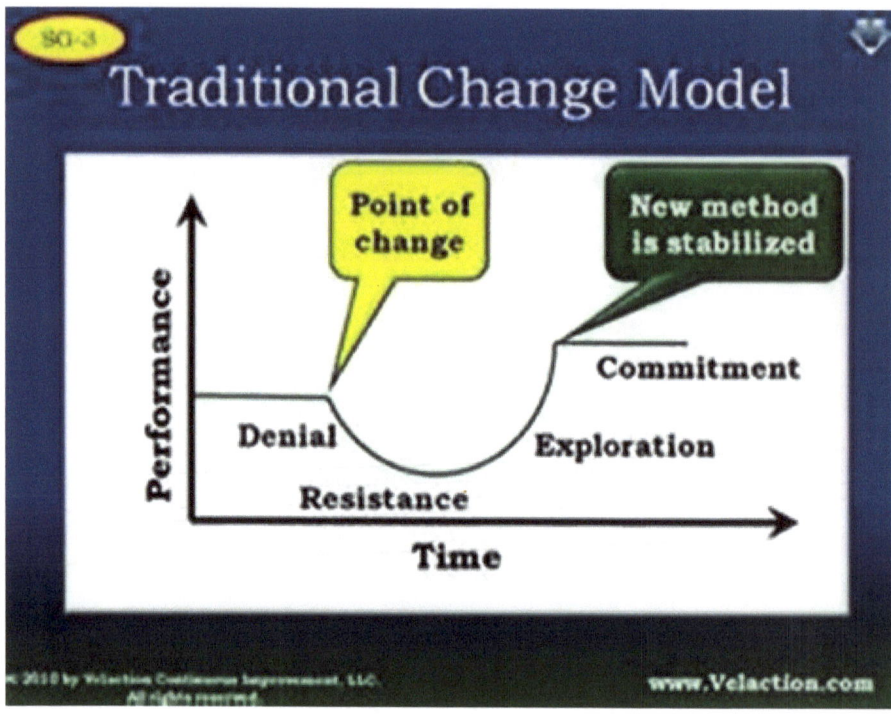

Traditional Change Model © Microsoft 2014

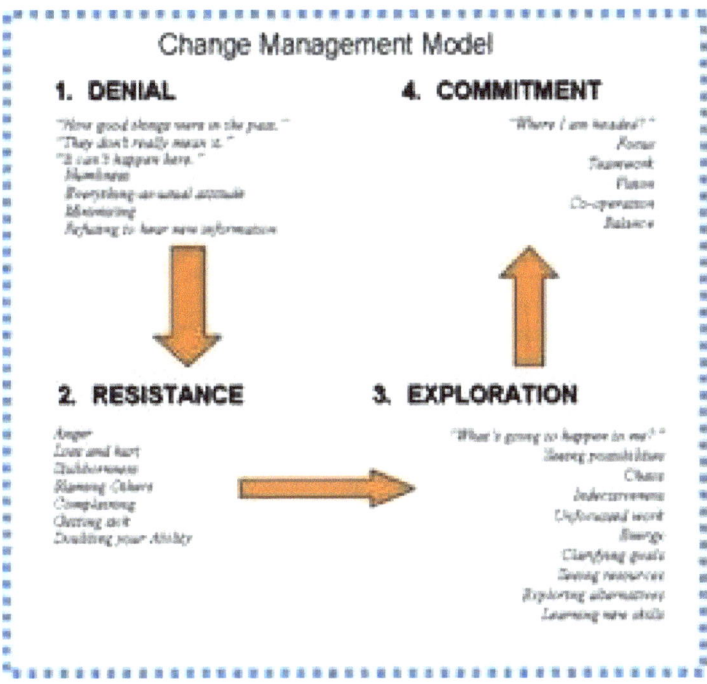

Change Management Model © Microsoft 2014

Theories that Address Effective Change Practices

Whilst discussing best practices for initiating organizational change, four theories will be briefly discussed: *ADKAR model, Kotter's Six Change Approach, Business Process Reengineering and Deming Cycle PDSA Model*; these theories have informed best practices in the initiation of organizational change.

ADKAR Model.

According to Kazmi & Naarananoja (2013) the ADKAR model was first presented by Prosci Research Inc. in 1998; this model focuses on the employee specific activities that will have an impact on the results of their tasks in their various organizations. The benefits to this model are mainly focused on the employee and the managers' ability to evaluate the causes of employee resistance to change. By evaluating the causal reasons for resisting change management can assist employees' transition through the process and also management can create and develop specific action plans to assist employees in embracing change (Kazmi & Naarananoja, 2013).

The ADKAR model focuses on employees, maintaining that success with the change plan will be apparent because the staff feels more involved in the process and will show more interest in the change process. The model is developed to be more tasks specific therefore results can be more easily evaluated and measured by management. Kazmi & Naaranaoja (2013) explained that the ADKAR model will work better with smaller companies. This is mainly because with this model larger companies will experience

difficulties putting into effect the ADKAR model. This model

requires working closely with employees and due to time constrains

and having the necessary resources to work closely with employees

it is better suited to a smaller company (Kazmi & Naaranaoja, 2013).

A	Awareness of the need for change	• Management communications • Customer input • Marketplace changes • Ready-access to information	
D	Desire to participate and support the change	• Fear of job loss • Discontent with current state • Imminent negative consequence • Enhanced job security • Affiliation and sense of belonging • Career advancement • Acquisition of power or position • Incentive or compensation • Trust and respect for leadership • Hope in future state	Enablers
K	Knowledge on how to change	• Training and education • Information access • Examples and role models	
A	Ability to implement required skills and behaviors	• Practice applying new skills or using new processes and tools • Coaching • Mentoring • Removal of barriers	
R	Reinforcement to sustain the change	• Incentives and rewards • Compensation changes • Celebrations • Personal recognition	

ADKAR Model © Microsoft 2014

Kotter Six Change Approach.

Applebaum et al. (2012) researched the Six Change Model

approach developed by Kotter which was developed as an approach

to negate the resistance to change by employees. This model was deemed to be a power model to incorporate into organizations of varying sizes (small, medium or large) because it covers numerous scenarios in the change management process - even issues that some organizations may never face because of their differences in size (Applebaum et al., 2012). This model surmises that management mainly reacts to the following factors of resistance from their employees: employees' interest of self-worth in the change process, employees may misunderstand communicating of the change process, employees may disapprove of the change process, and employee may not be in agreement with the reasoning for change within the organization.

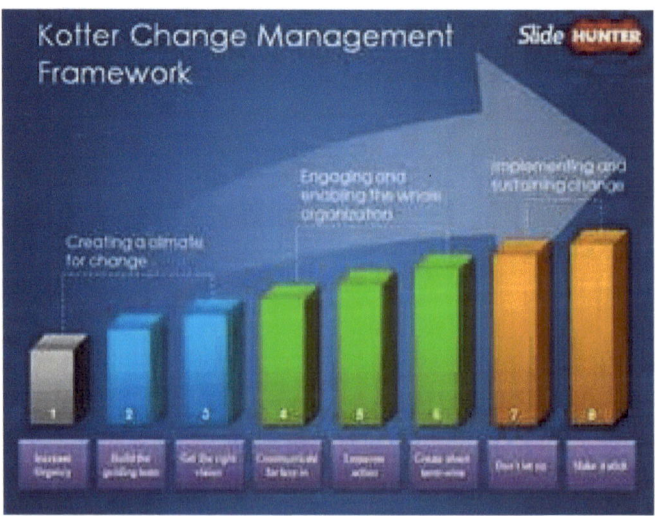

Kotter Model © Microsoft 2014

Business Process Reengineering.

According to Ozcelik (2009) reengineering is another effective and scientific form of change management. The term was conceptualized by Michael Hammer (1948-2008), and is a process of analyzing tools, introducing new techniques (training) and approaches, testing and validation to launch the change initiative. Business Process Reengineering theory is more focused on the employees output, outcomes, and the work process than on specific employee issues.

Ozcelik (2009) mentioned seven principles that can be used to streamline processes which in turn will improve cost, quality and time management increasing organizational productivity and efficiency. For organizations operating under low productivity and lacking effective management the business process reengineering theory/model is the efficient solution to reengineering its processes.

Business Process Reengineering © Microsoft 2014

Deming Cycle PDSA Model.

A final model for success as a change manager is the Deming Cycle

PDSA of continuous quality improvement. Young (2011) explained

that continuous quality improvement (CQI) is the classical work by

W. Edwards Deming (1900-1993), and is the reflection of what

exactly is needed in change management. The statistical evaluation

of the performance of a system and the removal of poorly

performing segments of that system identified after evaluation is the

key emphasis of CQI.

The essential elements according to Young (2011) are that

employees are constantly: **P**lanning, **D**oing, **S**tudying, and **A**cting

(PDSA). This, according to Young (2011), creates a culture in the

organization where the employee is always prepared for change and there is a constant movement towards change. With this model, strong functional teams are built, and employees become acceptable of the change process. This acceptance would then lead to employees being more attuned to the necessary changes within the process aiding in rapid organizational growth over time (Young, 2011).

Businesses continue to be interested in increasing the success rate of organizational change, and the literature has discussed best practices for initiating and implementing this type of change. These best practices will be discussed in the following chapter.

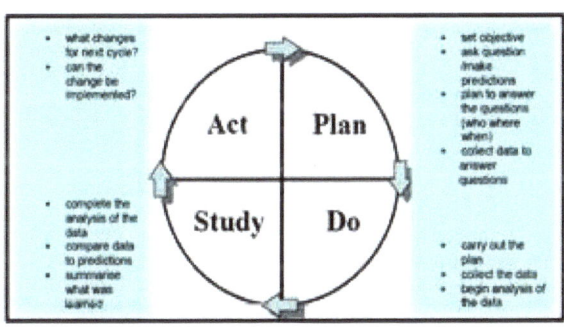

PDSA Model ©

Microsoft 2014

CHAPTER 2: Best Practices for Initiating Organizational Change

An organizational best practice has been defined in the literature as proven strategies and practices that drive organizational excellence (Heffes, 2002; Carter & Carmichael, 2009).The literature seems to suggest that there are some consistent best practices that can be applied to change initiation and management. These are related to managing communication; diversity; management's commitment to change; team building, and training.

Communication

Change management remains ineffectively executed in many businesses due to the lack of understanding of its major principles and the inability to communicate effectively (Choi, 2011). Understanding the basic tenets of change management and the significance of communication in the overall process remains crucial to ensure effective and smooth transitions caused by change (Choi, 2011). Management's ineffective communication of the company's intentions concerning change initiatives can lead to the loss of trust, growth of anxiety and insecurity among the workers, and this can result in resistance to change. Employees often feel excluded from the change process and resist change because of their doubts and insecurities about how the change will affect them (Lautner, 1999; Nelissen & Martine, 2008).

Poor communication can contribute to the failure of change initiatives; therefore, a best practice would be for management to communicate the nature of the change to employees, explain why it is needed, and how employees will be affected by the change (Lautner, 1999). This is however often neglected by executives who wrongly believe that change which can generate dramatic performance improvements will be welcomed without hesitation by the workers (Levesque, 2005). It is therefore imperative that management avoid making grand announcements about intended organizational changes without considering the effects of this on employees' emotional and cognitive reactions.

Communication of the vision, objectives, and goals of the company in the time of change will help to prevent growing insecurities among workers and can contribute to a smoother transition and encourage employees' support for change initiatives.

A best practice for initiating change would be to identify causes for employees' resistance to change and communicate clearly the need and purpose for the change so that employees would feel involved in the change process and would be less resistant to the change (Kazmi & Naarananoja, 2013)

Managing Diversity

Diversity has emerged as a challenge for management to handle effectively. Visagie, Linde, & Havenga (2011) asserted that effective diversity management is an absolute necessary leadership skill. A greater understanding of diversity and its role on organizational performance would underpin and even strengthen the process of initiating organizational change (Barak & Levin, 2002).

Barak and Levin (2002) emphasized that managing diversity has become a serious concern in the workplace because diverse views can cause conflicts of opinions, which can result in the lack of interest amongst employees regarding the achievements of organizational goals. Additionally, Barak and Levin (2002) maintained that the employee's feeling of isolation due to entrenched differences emerging from diversity result in their poor performance and unmet organizational goals. Therefore, the employee's social status is of paramount importance in improving organizational performance, and this should be attended to.

The literature has shown that lack of respect for diversity in the workplace results in discrimination, which contributes to conflicts, and stress and causes employee resistance to change initiatives. According to Ayoko et al. (2002), this issue can be addressed by introducing training in diversity and devising effective conflict resolution strategies. When organizations develop a culture of respect for diversity, employee interest in each other can result in a shared interest in supporting organizational goals, which include supporting the implementation of change initiatives

Teamwork and Training

As explained by Young (2011), and as Deming's PDSA model suggests, developing teams to work effectively together is another best practice for initiating organizational change. Sauer et al. (2006) and Bolt (2007) affirmed that team work is critical for the success of organizational performance in many technical and non-technical settings. Team relationships are based on interaction, and acceptance of team members' contribution to projects that support organizational goals. When conflicts arise between coworkers due to the tensions that characterize the working environment during the implementation of change management, stress, negativity, and resistance to change are the ultimate results.

Understanding the nature of conflict, its triggers, and effects is therefore essential to the ability to developing and managing teams and to minimize conflict at work. According to Bolt (2007) minimizing conflict at work can increase the satisfaction and harmonious atmosphere between coworkers. It is after all an established fact that conflicts between coworkers or workers and the management grow worse if left without resolution and this can be in its turn very costly to the organization (Bolt, 2007). As Ozcelik (2009) identified in the literature, training in new techniques contributed to positive employee outputs; additionally, educational sessions for the improvement of workers' communication skills and interaction is crucial in preparing employees to be receptive to change initiatives (Cloke, Goldsmith 2005).

Management commitment to change

In order to implement change successfully in an organization, Daft (2010) and Adams et al., (2006) maintained that there are key elements mandatory for the successful implementation of organizational change. These five elements, as outlined by Daft, are *idea, need, implementation, adoption, and resources*. For this purpose, organizational leadership occupies a crucial role because without their campaign and support for change, the organizational change cannot be enforced successfully; therefore, these five elements should be the paradigm of implementation processes for organizational leaders when introducing change (Daft, 2010). Erwin & Garman 2010 postulated that management, as proposers of change, must support change initiatives with the requisite resources, else employees will not support the change efforts. Some of these resources include training or re-training, and establishing and maintaining effective communication channels. It is also necessary for management to have in place the appropriate type of leadership to effectively guide the organization through the change process.

CHAPTER 3: Leader-follower Relationships in Change Management Strategy

In a discussion of leader-follower relationship in change management two leadership theories that are aligned with change management strategies will be discussed: *Transformational and Path Goal leadership theories.*

Transformational Theory.

According to Bommer et al., (2005) in relation to organizational change, transformational leadership is a democratic style of leadership that is concerned with principles of motivation, aspirations and integration of followers so as to achieve the ultimate goals of the organization. In transformational leadership theory, the leader works as a facilitator for followers and leads his followers towards decisions and solution of issues; additionally, these types of leaders are visionary and tend to devise policies that are aimed at long term goals. Oyinlade and Gellhaus (2005) highlighted the top ten essential behavioral leadership qualities for transformational leaders in organizational change management, which are: good communication skills, honest & ethical approach, fairness, and ability to motivate, provision of support aiding in decision-making, good interpersonal skills, problem-solving skills, strong organizational knowledge and good listening skills. Oyinlade & Gellhaus (2005) postulated that these aforementioned essential qualities are the major source of effective leadership and are to be found in principals of all successful organizations in the change management process.

Path goal theory.

According to Stogdill (1948) this contingency theory in organizational change management is an autocratic style of leadership that is considered a model for positive leadership. These leaders are perceived to be imbued with wisdom, intelligence and creativity (WIC). It was further suggested that this model of leadership could be attributed to any style of leadership, but was the core of positive leadership pertaining to managerial change.

In the seminal literature, Stogdill (1948) defined many traits associated with effective leadership that included intelligence, scholarship, dependability in practice of duties, activity and social involvement and superior socioeconomic status. According to Stogdill (1948) intelligence and effective leadership in change management were closely linked to each other. As far as the path-goal theory approach was concerned, leadership was contingent on two kinds of behaviors that were goal-oriented leading to output, and individual-oriented leading to personal goals achievement.

However, according to Hosmer (1995), for several reasons, the path-goal theory approach might not be appropriate for the business environment due to the disposition of employees' behaviors, the mixed composition of managers' behavioral approaches, and managers' naive natured behavioral approaches. Hosmer (1995) further stated that the path-goal theory of leadership did not accommodate individual differences in behavior, and also could not define the interaction between persons and situations.

Comparison and contrast of theories

Various proposals have been put forward to refresh the content of the two theories aiming to enhance their application for the management of change initiatives in organizations. It was suggested that there should be a link between the features of transformational leadership theory and path goal theory (House, 1996). The autocratic model of path-theory is meant to be a forceful style, while the democratic transformation model is referred to as an advisory leadership style. At the organizational level, goal-oriented tasks are achieved through these two styles of leadership, depending upon the situation requirements.

According to Ayoko et al. (2002), these two models both have a direct relation with job satisfaction because leaders choose leadership models on the basis of social circumstances; a forceful leadership style is demanding, directive and coercive in nature, while an advisory leadership style includes counseling, consultation and participation (Ayoko et. al, 2002). House (1996) emphasized that path-goal theory of leadership should be avoided, and value-based leadership, such as transformational leadership, should be highly encouraged to achieve effective leadership. The major speculation about the relation between path-goal and transformational leadership has been the difference between them pertaining to achieving improved performance of followers (House, 1996). For example, path-goal leadership is directive and autocratic in nature, whilst transformational leadership is supportive and democratic.

Several proposals have been offered to make the two theories more comprehensive and concise by expanding their content in such a way that will indicatively lead to effective change management (Vecchio et al., 2008). As far as theoretical and practical approaches of supportive and directive styles of leadership are concerned, a significant difference was detectable between the path-goal and transformational theories of leadership.

Since the employment environment has been changing tremendously, organizations need to train their employees in order to cope with contemporary challenges (such as diversity) so that they may be able to survive against the variable situations of employment. Bass' 1985 model of transformational leadership suggests that when leaders furnish followers with the appropriate skills, followers can succeed in these challenging business environments (Rafferty & Griffin, 2006; Bass, 1990).

Leaders have a direct impact on the behavioral psychology of followers, and this is routed through the climate of the working environment (Rotmans & Loorbach, 2009). Some theorists have postulated that motivation and performance can only be enhanced by effective leadership, which can be achieved through path-goal leadership theory, while others have endorsed transformational theory.

CHAPTER 4: Discussion

Change must not only be well-managed, but also planned, organized, directed, and controlled. Change requires effective and structured leadership; particularly a leadership that is capable of formulating a coherent and motivational vision, strategy, and organizational culture based on shared and sustainable values (Gill 2003, p. 307).

According to Levesque (2005) change management starts long before the actual change itself is implemented. The seminal literature has shown that as far back as 1911 the scientific management of change was recommended. Daft (2010) and Soparnot (2011) pioneered new yet vocal concepts of organizational change by aligning innovation with organizational theory. Pointing towards contemporary challenges, Both Daft (2010) and Soparnot (2011) observed that organizations are currently undergoing serious economic turmoil in the US and other developed countries.

Advances in technology remain at the heart of competition in organizations, and the intensity of the competition is growing with the passage of time. This phenomenon of change holds the promise of massive benefits for the adoption of technological advancements can give early adopters a competitive edge over the competition Soparnot (2011). It is essential that the further additions or updates in the organization theory should be inclusive of innovation, sustainability, and the required level of adaptability and validity. However, there are diverse and conflicting views about organizational change theory.

The seminal and contemporary literature recommended that, in order to decrease conflicting views, organizations should consider developing organizational structures that could be aligned with contemporary trends and challenges for an enhanced compatibility (McKinley, Mone, & Moon, 1999; Mintzberg, Ahlstrand & Lampel, 2005).

Summary

The path-goal theory of leadership emphasized the interaction between leader's trait and the situation surrounding the leader. On the other hand, the literature has shown that transformational leadership is highly effective; however, it is not advised for those organizations that are already working successfully (Stenberg, 2005). Leaders and followers must be aware of limitations in situations in order to avoid any conflict in their approaches, and leaders must provide the followers with the resources for career achievement and self-satisfaction (Gunbayi, 2005).

Change Management

Conclusion

This book analyzed and discussed the best practices for initiating organizational change, and evaluated how leader-follower relationships can affect the change management strategy. In order to successfully implement change initiatives in organizations, Daft (2010) maintained that five key elements would serve the purpose. These five elements are *idea, need, implementation, adoption and resources*. To support these elements, five best practices for successfully managing organizational change were proposed: communication, management of teams, and management of diversity within the organization, training, and managerial support for change.

The literature showed that effective communication and appropriate training and development initiatives can help to allay employees' fears and improve interaction among diverse team members and also between leadership and workers, which can result in the desired organizational goals. It was found that leadership has a direct impact on the behavioral psychology of followers, and is routed through the climate of the working environment. In other words, employee motivation and performance can only be enhanced by effective leadership. It was found that leadership styles that were informed by path-goal theory and transformational leadership were helpful in effectively initiating organizational change, depending on the value of the change; however, transformational leadership was more effective when high value change was implemented.

Change © Microsoft 2014

REFERENCES

Adams, R., Bessant, J., & Phelps, R. (2006). Innovation management measurement: A

review. *International Journal of Management Reviews, 8*(1), 21-47.

doi:10.1111/j.1468-2370.2006.00119.x

Appelbaum, S. H., Habashy, S., Malo, J., & Shafiq, H. (2012). Back to the future: Revisiting

Kotter's 1996 change model. *The Journal of Management Development, 31*(8), 764-782.

doi:http://dx.doi.org/10.1108/02621711211253231

Ayoko, O. B., Hartel, C. E. J. & Callan, V. J. (2002). Resolving the puzzle of productive and destructive conflict in culturally heterogeneous workgroups: A communication accommodation theory approach. *The International Journal of Conflict Management, 13(2),* 165-195.

Barak, M. E. M. & Levin, A. (2002). Outside of the corporate mainstream and excluded from the work community: a study of diversity, job satisfaction and well-being. *Community, Work and Family, 5(2),* 133-157.

Bass, B.M. (1990). From transactional to transformational leadership. *Organizational Dynamics, 18*(3), 19-32.

Bommer, W. H., Rich, G. A., & Rubin, R. S. (2005). Changing attitudes about change: longitudinal effects of transformational leader behavior on employee cynicism about organizational change. *Journal of Organizational Behavior, 26*(7), 733-753. doi:10.1002/job.342

Blake, A. M., & Moseley, J. L. (2011). Frederick Winslow Taylor: One hundred years of managerial insight. *International Journal of Management, 28*(4), 346-353. Retrieved from http://search.proquest.com.library.capella.edu/docview/1008 666375?accountid=27965

Bolt, S. (2007). The challenge of integrating research, action and learning in the workplace to affect organizational change. *International Journal of Pedagogies & Learning, 3*(2), 42 - 51

Carter, L., & Carmichael, P. (2009). Best practices. *Leadership Excellence, 26*(11), 16-17. Retrieved from http://search.proquest.com.library.capella.edu/docview/2046 23890?accountid=27965

Choi, M. (2011). Employees' attitudes toward organizational change: A literature review. *Human Resource Management, 50*(4), 479-500. doi:10.1002/hrm.20434

Daft, R. L. (2010). *Organization theory and design* (10th ed.). Mason, OH: South-Western Cengage Learning.

Davis, G. F. & Marquis, C. (2005). Prospects for organization theory in the early twenty-first century: Institutional fields and mechanisms. *Organization Science, 16*(4), 332-343.

Erwin, D. G., & Garman, A. N. (2010). Resistance to organizational change: Linking research and practice. *Leadership & Organization Development Journal, 31*(1), 39-56. doi:http://dx.doi.org/10.1108/01437731011010371

Giannantonio, C. M., PhD. & Hurley-Hanson, A. (2011). Frederick Winslow Taylor: Reflections on the relevance of the principles of scientific management 100 years later. *Journal of Business and Management, 17*(1), 7-10. Retrieved from http://search.proquest.com.library.capella.edu/docview/1011 816590?accountid=27965

Gumusluoglu, L. & Ilsev, A. (2009). Transformational leadership, creativity, and organizational innovation. *Journal of Business Research, 62* (4), 461–473.

http://dx.doi.org/10.1016/j.jbusres.2007.07.032

Harwood, S. A. (2012). The management of change and the viplan methodology in practice. *The Journal of the Operational Research Society, 63*(6), 748-761. doi:http://dx.doi.org/10.1057/jors.2011.73

Heffes, E. M. (2002). Best practices...by definition. *Financial Executive, 18*(2), 44-45. Retrieved from http://search.proquest.com.library.capella.edu/docview/2088 87820?accountid=27965

Hosmer, L. T. (1995). Trust: The connecting link between organizational theory and philosophical ethics. *The Academy of Management Review, 20*(2), 379-403.

House, R. J. (1996). Path-goal theory of leadership: Lessons, legacy, and a reformulated theory. *Leadership Quarterly. 7*(3), 323–352.

Kazmi, S. A. Z., & Naarananoja, M. (2013). Collection of change management models - an

opportunity to make the best choice from the various organizational transformational

techniques. *GSTF Business Review* (GBR), *2*(4), 44-57. Retrieved from

http://search.proquest.com.library.capella.edu/docview/1437 608476?accountid=27965

Nelissen, P., & Martine, V. S. (2008). Surviving organizational change: How management communication helps balance mixed feelings. *Corporate Communications, 13*(3), 306-318. doi:http://dx.doi.org/10.1108/13563280810893670

Nelson, D. (1980). *Taylor and scientific management.* Madison, WI: The University of Wisconsin Press.

Ozcelik, Y (2009). Do business process reengineering projects payoff? Evidence from the United

States. *International Journal of Project Management, 28*(1), 7–13.

Retrieved from http://dx.doi.org/10.1016/j.ijproman.2009.03.004

Preget, L. (2013). Understanding organizational change as an interactional accomplishment: A conversation analytic approach. *Journal of Change Management, 13*(3), 338 - 361. Retrieved from http://search.proquest.com.library.capella.edu/docview/1438 894145?accountid=27965

Raineri, B.A. (2011). Change management practices: Impact on perceived change results. *Journal of Business Research, 64* (3), 266–272.

Rotmans, J., & Loorbach, D. (2009). Complexity and transition management. *Journal of*

Industrial Ecology, 13(2), 184-196. doi:10.1111/j.1530-9290.2009.00116.x

Sauer, J., Felsing, T., Franke, H. & Ruttinger, B. (2006). Cognitive diversity and team performance in a complex multiple task environment. *Ergonomics, 49*(10), 934-954.

Soparnot, R. (2011). The concept of organizational change capacity. *Journal of Organizational Change Management, 24*(5), 640-661. doi:http://dx.doi.org/10.1108/09534811111158903

Stogdill, R. M. (1948). Personal factors associated with leadership: A survey of the

literature. *Journal of Psychology, 25* (1), 35–71. doi:http://dx.doi.org/: 10.1080/00223980.1948.9917362

Taylor, F. W. (1911). *The principles of scientific management and testimony before the special house committee.* New York, NY: Harper & Row.

Visagie, J., Linde, H., & Havenga, W. (2011). Leadership competencies for managing diversity. *Managing Global Transitions, 9*(3), 225-247. Retrieved from http://search.proquest.com.library.capella.edu/docview/9056 58431?accountid=27965

Young, M. (2011). The continuous improvement grid: An empirical investigation into the

effectiveness of a systems, and action research, based continuous improvement intervention, for 'new' organization development. *Systemic Practice and Action Research,*

24(5), 453-478. Retrieved from doi:http://dx.doi.org/10.1007/s11213-011-9195-7.

Appendix

All images for Change Management, Organization Management and Change Management Models are courtesy Microsoft

©Microsoft 2014